DINOSAUR DIG

Dinosaur Families

Unearth the secrets behind dinosaur fossils

QED

QED Publishing

Rupert Matthews

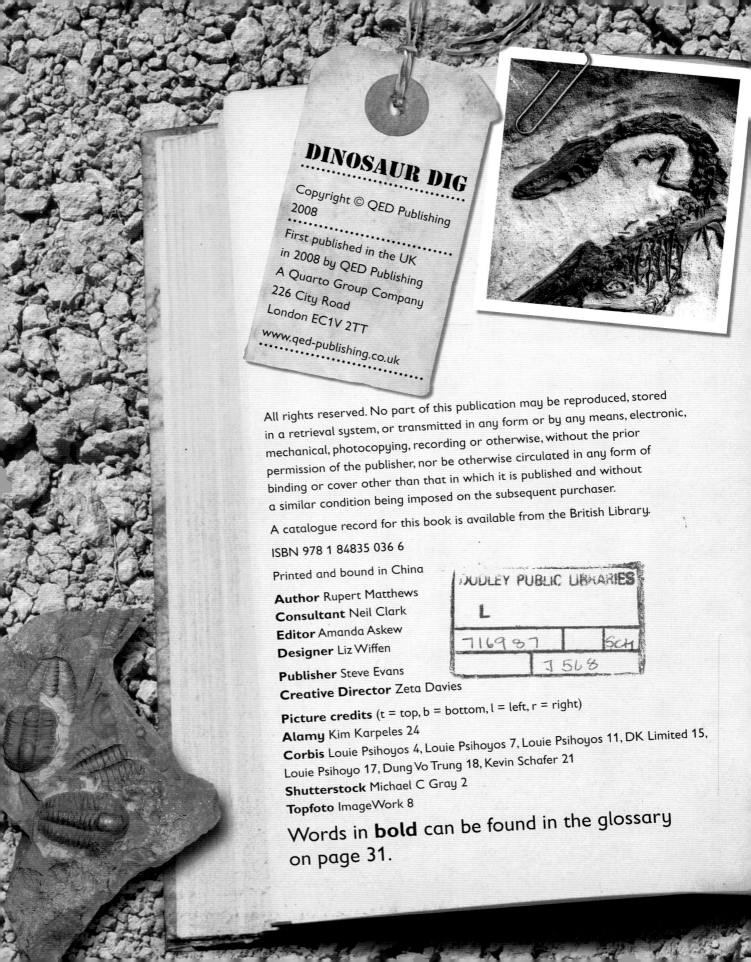

DINOSAUR DIG

Copyright © QED Publishing 2008

First published in the UK in 2008 by QED Publishing
A Quarto Group Company
226 City Road
London EC1V 2TT

www.qed-publishing.co.uk

A catalogue record for this book is available from the British Library.

ISBN 978 1 84835 036 6

Printed and bound in China

Author Rupert Matthews
Consultant Neil Clark
Editor Amanda Askew
Designer Liz Wiffen

Publisher Steve Evans
Creative Director Zeta Davies

Picture credits (t = top, b = bottom, l = left, r = right)
Alamy Kim Karpeles 24
Corbis Louie Psihoyos 4, Louie Psihoyos 7, Louie Psihoyos 11, DK Limited 15, Louie Psihoyo 17, Dung Vo Trung 18, Kevin Schafer 21
Shutterstock Michael C Gray 2
Topfoto ImageWork 8

Words in **bold** can be found in the glossary on page 31.

CONTENTS

DINO GUIDE

For every dinosaur in this book and many more, learn how to pronounce their name, find out their length and weight, and discover what they ate.

DINOSAUR DIG

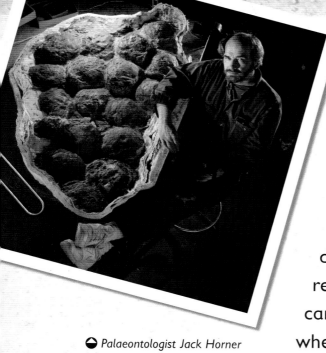

Dinosaurs **were** reptiles **that lived on Earth. They became** extinct **about 65 million years ago. There are no dinosaurs alive today.**

Scientists called **palaeontologists** (pay-lee-on-toll-oh-jists) study dinosaurs. By examining dinosaur remains, called **fossils**, palaeontologists can show what dinosaurs looked like when they were alive.

◗ *Palaeontologist Jack Horner has excavated, or dug up, a nest of fossilized dinosaur eggs in the USA.*

1 A dinosaur dies on a lakeshore

2

3

The **skeleton** sinks into the lake

Many dinosaur remains have been found – of **adults**, youngsters, babies and even of eggs in nests. These remains help palaeontologists to understand how dinosaur families lived and behaved.

⬤ *When a plant or animal dies, it usually rots away completely. However, in special conditions, parts of it can become fossilized.*

4 Layers of mud settle over the skeleton. The mud and bones gradually turn into stone

The rock wears away, or **erodes**

5 As more rock erodes, the skeleton is revealed

CARING FOR THE EGGS

Dinosaurs laid eggs, which were kept warm and safe until they hatched into babies.

In hot areas, the eggs were laid on the warm ground. The mother dinosaur would stay nearby to provide shade from the sun if the eggs became too hot.

In cooler parts of the world, the mother dinosaur may have piled leaves on top of the eggs. As the leaves rotted, they produced heat, which kept the eggs warm.

DINOSAUR DIG
Jobaria

WHERE: Niger, Africa

PERIOD: 110 million years ago in the early Cretaceous

DIG SITE

WOW!

In July 1923, Roy Chapman Andrews and his team found the first dinosaur eggs in Mongolia, Asia — they were *Oviraptor* (oh-vee-rap-tor) eggs.

Jobaria

20 metres in length

This model shows a baby dinosaur inside its egg. The baby feeds on the sac, or bag, of orange yolk. It breathes the oxygen that filters through the egg shell.

A mother Jobaria (joe-barr-ee-ah) tries to drive off a smaller hunting dinosaur. Many dinosaur eggs were eaten before they had a chance to hatch.

THE NURSERY

DINOSAUR DIG
Maiasaura

WHERE: Montana, North America

PERIOD: 75 million years ago in the late Cretaceous

DIG SITE

Some dinosaurs built large nurseries where more than 100 dinosaurs laid their eggs in nests close to each other.

After the eggs hatched, the adult dinosaurs brought food to their young and guarded the nursery from attack. The babies stayed in the nest for several weeks.

Hunting dinosaurs may have cared for their babies in a similar way. Young hunters probably followed their parents for several months so that they could learn how to hunt successfully.

◐ Maiasaura *(my-yah-saw-rah)* *would hatch from their eggs* *after eight to ten weeks.*

⬭ *The young Maiasaura stayed in the nursery for several weeks after they hatched, so they could be cared for by their parents.*

WOW!

Maiasaura was the first dinosaur with a female name. Most dinosaur names end in 'us', which shows that they are male names.

Maiasaura

9 metres in length

YOUNGSTERS

Young animals, including dinosaurs, look and behave differently from adults.

Their head and eyes are large in proportion to their body – this makes their body look too small! Their legs tend to be shorter and thicker than those of adults.

Mussaurus (muss-saw-rus) had a large head, large eyes and short legs. Scientists think that the fossil they have found is of a baby animal. The adult would have been much larger and looked different.

🔨 DIG SITE

◗ *A baby Mussaurus would only have been 20 centimetres in length – about the size of a rat.*

WOW!

Fossils of a young *Tyrannosaurus* (tie-rann-oh-saw-rus) have been found. The remains show that it was probably a fierce killer, just like the adult.

Mussaurus

4 metres in length

⬤ The fossil of Mussaurus is one of the smallest dinosaur skeletons ever found, but it is of a baby. The adult would have been about 4 metres in length.

LEAVING THE NEST

Not all dinosaurs cared for their young in nurseries. Some youngsters had to look after themselves.

Young **sauropods**, such as *Apatosaurus* (ap-at-oh-saw-rus), hid from hunters in bushes and other **undergrowth**. As they grew larger, the youngsters may have left the safety of cover as they were able to fight off attackers.

Fossil footprints show that sauropods waded into lakes or rivers. They may have been hiding or escaping from hunters.

DINOSAUR DIG
Apatosaurus

WHERE: Wyoming, North America

PERIOD: 150 million years ago in the late Jurassic

DIG SITE

Apatosaurus

25 metres in length

● Young sauropods, such as Apatosaurus, left the nest when they were only a few days old. Adults collected soft plants for the babies to eat when they hatched, but then they ignored their young.

WOW!

Fossils of *Apatosaurus* came from rocks of the Morrison Formation, USA. These contain more dinosaur fossils than any other rocks on Earth.

13

LIFE SKILLS

Some scientists believe that baby dinosaurs sometimes followed their parents instead of living by themselves.

A young dinosaur relied on its parent for protection against attack. The youngster would have learned many skills by watching its parent, including which plants were good to eat, which food to avoid, and which dinosaurs were dangerous hunters.

WOW!

In 1868, a complete Cetiosaurus skeleton was discovered by English palaeontologist, Sir Richard Owen.

◑ *The backbone of Cetiosaurus (set-ee-oh-saw-rus) looks similar to a whale's, which is why the creature was given a name that means 'whale lizard'. At first, scientists thought Cetiosaurus was a sea animal, until fossils of the leg bones were found.*

Cetiosaurus

18 metres in length

◑ *A young Cetiosaurus follows its parent across open ground. The adult would protect its young as well as teaching it how to survive.*

UNDER ATTACK

Some dinosaurs lived together in groups called herds. The fully grown adults would join together to protect the youngsters.

Herds of animals work together. If a hunter, such as *Tyrannosaurus* (tie-rann-oh-saw-rus), threatened to attack a herd of *Triceratops* (try-ser-ah-tops), they would form a circle.

The adults stood on the outside of the circle with their sharp horns facing outwards to protect the youngsters standing on the inside. *Tyrannosaurus* would be unable to reach the young, so it would give up the hunt and leave.

DINOSAUR DIG

Triceratops
Tyrannosaurus

WHERE: Colorado, North America

PERIOD: 65 million years ago in the late Cretaceous

DIG SITE

WOW!

Scientists have found 20 *Tyrannosaurus* skeletons – more than of any other large hunting dinosaur.

◑ *Tyrannosaurus* could not break into a circle of defending *Triceratops*. However, it may return later to try to grab a youngster by surprise.

Tyrannosaurus

12 metres in length

A complete fossilized skeleton of Triceratops. Its large horns may have been used to fight other dinosaurs, including hunters.

Triceratops

9 metres in length

GOING IT ALONE

As a young dinosaur grew older, it would become stronger and begin to learn the skills it needed to survive.

Eventually a youngster would be able to look after itself. Instead of following its parent everywhere, the youngster may gradually start to drift away and begin to live on its own.

Iguanodon (ig-wan-oh-don) fed on shrubs and small trees. A young *Iguanodon* may stay with its parent for a year or two before it left to live by itself.

DINOSAUR DIG
Iguanodon

WHERE: England, Europe

WHEN: 140 million years ago in the early Cretaceous

DIG SITE

◑ *An adult* Iguanodon *jawbone. A youngster would have had a similar jaw and teeth as it ate the same food.*

Iguanodon

10 metres in length

◑ *A young* Iguanodon *tries to keep up with its parent. The adult dinosaur would gradually lose interest in its young as it grew older. Eventually they would separate.*

THREAT DISPLAYS

Adults may have been forced to compete with other dinosaurs of the same type.

If there was little food, survival depended on finding good feeding grounds. It is thought that some hunters may have had a home area, or territory, where they would not allow others of their kind to hunt.

DINOSAUR DIG
Dilophosaurus

WHERE: Arizona, North America

WHEN: 190 million years ago in the early Jurassic

DIG SITE

WOW!

The bones in the crests of Dilophosaurus were as thin as paper in places.

Dilophosaurus (die-low-fo-saw-rus) had a pair of bony **crests** growing from the top of its **skull**. Scientists believe that the dinosaur may have used these crests in a threat display to scare away hunters.

◑ *This fossil of Dilophosaurus is almost complete, although some of the bones have become mixed up. The crests on its head can clearly be seen.*

◑ *A pair of rival Dilophosaurus display their crests to each other by pacing back and forth. A fight would only take place if neither dinosaur backed down.*

Dilophosaurus

6 metres in length

POWER STRUGGLE

Sometimes threats and displays would not settle a struggle between dinosaurs. They would often fight to decide which was the strongest.

Stegoceras (steg-oh-sair-ass) was a **bonehead** dinosaur. It had a very thick skull with a dome of solid bone on top of its head. Some scientists think that *Stegoceras* fought each other using their heads.

DINOSAUR DIG
Stegoceras

WHERE: Montana, North America

WHEN: 75 million years ago in the late Cretaceous

DIG SITE

⬤ *Stegoceras fought by charging towards each other. The force used when they crashed together would soon show which dinosaur was the strongest.*

WOW!

Stegoceras skulls could be as much as 8 centimetres in thickness. Males had thicker skulls than females.

Stegoceras would run at each other with their heads lowered. They would crash together with enormous force. After a few impacts, the weaker dinosaur would give up the fight. Scientists believe that they probably hit each other on the sides of the body, rather than head-butting.

Stegoceras

2 metres in length

HERD INSTINCT

Some sauropods, such as *Mamenchisaurus* (ma-men-key-saw-rus), lived in herds – from as few as ten dinosaurs to as many as 100.

Living in a herd had advantages because one or two dinosaurs would always be looking out for danger. The dinosaurs could join forces to drive off a hunter. In a herd, plant eaters could find water or good eating grounds more easily.

DIG SITE

◑ *Mamenchisaurus may have been able to rear up on its back legs, using the tail to balance. Then Mamenchisaurus could feed on even higher leaves on trees.*

Mamenchisaurus

24 metres in length

WOW!

Mamenchisaurus had the longest neck of any dinosaur. It was more than 10 metres in length – that's the same as six people lying end to end.

● A herd of sauropods wanders across a dry plain. Fossil footprints show that younger animals stayed in the centre of the herd where they would be protected from attack.

THE END OF THE STORY

All dinosaurs eventually died. Some were killed by hunters or died after a fight. Others fell victim to disease or to an accident. Some probably just died of old age.

Leaellynasaura (lee-ell-in-ah-saw-rah) lived in Australia. Millions of years ago, the winters would have been very cold. If *Leaellynasaura* could not keep warm enough, it may have died from the cold.

When a dinosaur died, its body was most likely either to be eaten by the first hunter to find it or to rot away completely. The bones or teeth of only a few creatures remained as fossils.

A dinosaur that died next to a river had a better chance of being fossilized as its body would have been quickly covered by mud or sand.

DINOSAUR DIG
Leaellynasaura

WHERE: Victoria, Australia

WHEN: 110 million years ago in the mid Cretaceous

DIG SITE

WOW!

A large number of bones has been found in Alberta, Canada. Scientists believe that hundreds of dinosaurs were swept away by a fast-flowing river.

A dead Leaellynasaura lies beside a frozen river. It is thought that the long, cold winters may have killed off many weaker dinosaurs.

Leaellynasaura

2 metres in length

DINO GUIDE

Coelophysis

PRONUNCIATION see-low-fye-sis

LENGTH 3 metres

WEIGHT 35 kilograms

DIET Small animals

Efraasia

PRONUNCIATION ef-rah-see-ah

LENGTH 7 metres

WEIGHT 600 kilograms

DIET Plants

Eoraptor

PRONUNCIATION ee-oh-rap-tor

LENGTH 1 metre

WEIGHT 3–15 kilograms

DIET Small animals

Herrerasaurus

PRONUNCIATION he-ray-ra-saw-rus

LENGTH 3 metres

WEIGHT 200 kilograms

DIET Animals

Melanorosaurus

PRONUNCIATION mel-an-or-oh-saw-rus

LENGTH 10 metres

WEIGHT 1 tonne

DIET Plants

Mussaurus (p10)

PRONUNCIATION muss-saw-rus

LENGTH 4 metres (adult)

WEIGHT 150 kilograms

DIET Plants

Pisanosaurus

PRONUNCIATION peez-an-oh-saw-rus

LENGTH 1 metre

WEIGHT 3 kilograms

DIET Plants

Plateosaurus

PRONUNCIATION plat-ee-oh-saw-rus

LENGTH 8 metres

WEIGHT 1 tonne

DIET Plants

Riojasaurus

PRONUNCIATION ree-oh-ha-saw-rus

LENGTH 10 metres

WEIGHT 1 tonne

DIET Plants

Staurikosaurus

PRONUNCIATION store-ick-oh-saw-rus

LENGTH 2 metres

WEIGHT 30 kilograms

DIET Small animals

JURASSIC PERIOD
206 TO 145 MILLION YEARS AGO

Allosaurus
PRONUNCIATION
al-oh-saw-rus
LENGTH 12 metres
WEIGHT 1.5–2 tonnes
DIET Animals

Apatosaurus (p12)
PRONUNCIATION
ap-at-oh-saw-rus
LENGTH 25 metres
WEIGHT 25–35 tonnes
DIET Plants

Ceratosaurus
PRONUNCIATION
se-rat-oh-saw-rus
LENGTH 6 metres
WEIGHT 700–850 kilograms
DIET Animals

Cetiosaurus (p14)
PRONUNCIATION
set-ee-oh-saw-rus
LENGTH 18 metres
WEIGHT 15–20 tonnes
DIET Plants

Dilophosaurus (p20)
PRONUNCIATION
die-low-fo-saw-rus
LENGTH 6 metres
WEIGHT 400 kilograms
DIET Animals

Mamenchisaurus (p24)
PRONUNCIATION
ma-men-key-saw-rus
LENGTH 24 metres
WEIGHT 12–15 tonnes
DIET Plants

Megalosaurus
PRONUNCIATION
meg-ah-low-saw-rus
LENGTH 9 metres
WEIGHT 1 tonne
DIET Plants

Ornitholestes
PRONUNCIATION
or-nith-oh-less-teez
LENGTH 2 metres
WEIGHT 30 kilograms
DIET Animals

Sinosauropteryx
PRONUNCIATION
sy-no-saw-op-tur-iks
LENGTH 1 metre
WEIGHT 3 kilograms
DIET Small animals

Stegosaurus
PRONUNCIATION
steg-oh-saw-rus
LENGTH 8–9 metres
WEIGHT 2–3 tonnes
DIET Plants

CRETACEOUS PERIOD
145 TO 65 MILLION YEARS AGO

Euoplocephalus

PRONUNCIATION
you-oh-ploe-sef-ah-lus
LENGTH 6–7 metres
WEIGHT 2 tonnes
DIET Plants

Iguanodon (p18)
PRONUNCIATION
ig-wan-oh-don
LENGTH 10 metres
WEIGHT 4–5 tonnes
DIET Plants

Jobaria (p6)
PRONUNCIATION
joe-barr-ee-ah
LENGTH 20 metres
WEIGHT 18–20 tonnes
DIET Plants

Leaellynasaura (p26)

PRONUNCIATION
lee-ell-in-ah-saw-rah
LENGTH 2 metres
WEIGHT 10 kilograms
DIET Plants

Maiasaura (p8)
PRONUNCIATION
my-yah-saw-rah
LENGTH 9 metres
WEIGHT 3–4 tonnes
DIET Plants

Monoclonius

PRONUNCIATION
mon-oh-clone-ee-us
LENGTH 5 metres
WEIGHT 2–3 tonnes
DIET Plants

Oviraptor (p6)

PRONUNCIATION
oh-vee-rap-tor
LENGTH 2 metres
WEIGHT 30 kilograms
DIET Small animals and plants

Stegoceras (p22)

PRONUNCIATION
steg-oh-sair-ass
LENGTH 2 metres
WEIGHT 50–70 kilograms
DIET Plants

Triceratops (p16)

PRONUNCIATION
try-ser-ah-tops
LENGTH 9 metres
WEIGHT 5–8 tonnes
DIET Plants

Tyrannosaurus (p16)

PRONUNCIATION
tie-rann-oh-saw-rus
LENGTH 12 metres
WEIGHT 6 tonnes
DIET Large animals

GLOSSARY

Adult An animal that is fully grown.

Bonehead A type of dinosaur that had a thick layer of bone on top of its skull.

Crest Bone on the top of the head.

Cretaceous The third period of time in the age of the dinosaurs. The Cretaceous began about 145 million years ago and ended about 65 million years ago.

Dinosaur A type of reptile that lived millions of years ago. All dinosaurs are now extinct.

Erode To wear away.

Extinct Not existing any more. An animal is extinct when they have all died out.

Fossil Any part of a plant or animal that has been preserved in rock. Also traces of plants or animals, such as footprints.

Hatch To emerge from an egg.

Herd A group of animals that lives together.

Jurassic The second period of time in the age of the dinosaurs. The Jurassic began about 206 million years ago and ended about 145 million years ago.

Nursery A place where dinosaurs went to hatch their babies and where the young lived for some time afterwards.

Palaeontologist A scientist who studies ancient forms of life, including dinosaurs.

Reptile A cold-blooded animal, such as a lizard. Dinosaurs were reptiles, too.

Sauropod A type of dinosaur that had a long neck and tail. Sauropods included the largest of all dinosaurs.

Skeleton The bones in an animal's body.

Skull The bones of the head of an animal. The skull does not include the jaw, but many skulls have jaws attached.

Triassic The first period of time in the age of the dinosaurs. The Triassic began about 248 million years ago and ended about 208 million years ago.

Undergrowth Bushes, small trees and other plants that grow under bigger plants and trees.

INDEX